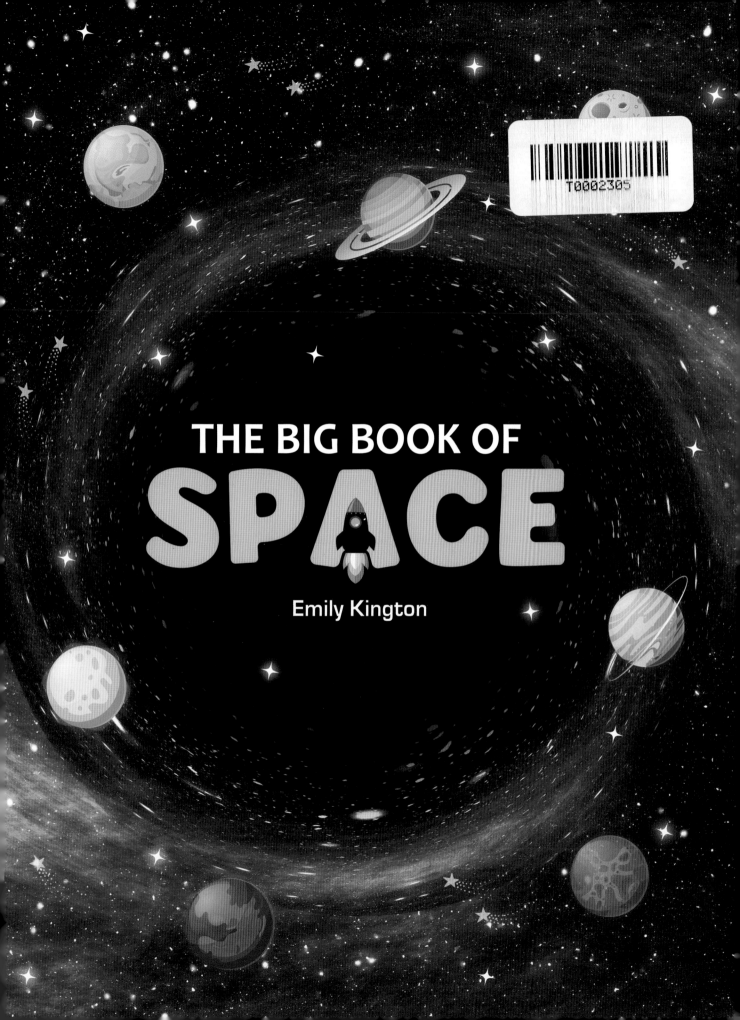

THE BIG BOOK OF
SPACE

Emily Kington

First published in 2022 by
Hungry Tomato Ltd
F1, Old Bakery Studios,
Malpas Road, Truro,
Cornwall, TR1 1QH, UK.

Copyright © 2022 Hungry Tomato Ltd.

Beetle Books is an imprint
of Hungry Tomato.

A CIP catalog record for this book is
available from the British Library.

ISBN 978-1-913440-97-8

Printed and bound in China.

Discover more at
www.mybeetlebooks.com
www.hungrytomato.com

Words that appear in **bold** are explained in the glossary.

Contents

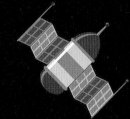

What Is the Universe?

The universe is the whole of space and everything that exists within it. Scientists believe that it is getting bigger all the time.

It's not just planets, stars and dust clouds that make up the universe. All living things on Earth, including every plant that grows, is part of it, too!

It is impossible to know how big the universe actually is. It is so big that we will never be able to discover it all.

The universe is thought to be 13.73 billion years old!

Many scientists believe that the universe was created by a massive explosion known as the *Big Bang*.

5

The Solar System

The solar system contains all of the planets, dwarf planets, moons, and other objects that travel around the Sun.

A planet's journey around the Sun is called an **orbit**. Planets stay in orbit because of a pulling force from the Sun, called **gravity**.

Mercury

Venus

There are eight planets in the solar system, including Earth.

Neptune

Uranus

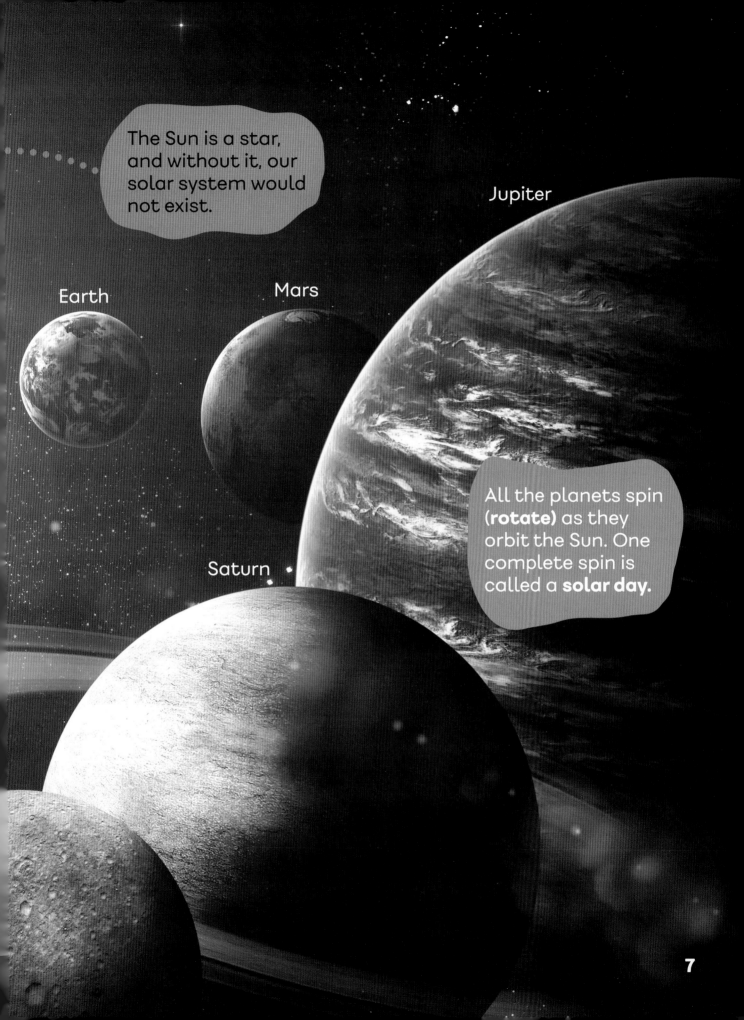

The Sun is a star, and without it, our solar system would not exist.

Jupiter

Earth

Mars

All the planets spin (**rotate**) as they orbit the Sun. One complete spin is called a **solar day.**

Saturn

Mercury

Mercury is often considered to be the closest planet to Earth. Although Venus gets closer, it only sweeps by us. Mercury remains nearer for longer.

A solar day on Mercury, the smallest planet, is 1,408 hours long!

Mercury is the fastest planet to orbit the Sun. Speeding at about 107,000 miles per hour (172,200 km/h), it only takes about 88 days.

Mercury is also the closest planet to the Sun.

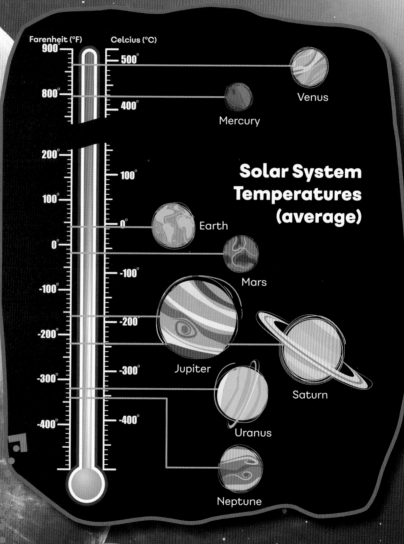

Solar System Temperatures (average)

Sun

Mercury

Venus

Earth

Mars

Jupiter

Saturn

Uranus

Neptune

Daytime temperatures on Mercury can reach 800°F (427°C). It's unlikely that we would ever be able to live there!

Venus

Venus is hotter than Mercury, even though it is farther away from the Sun. It takes just over 224 days to orbit the Sun.

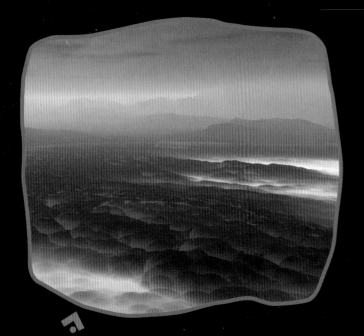

It is so hot on Venus that it would turn metals, such as lead, into liquid!

Venus rotates in the opposite direction to the other planets.

You can sometimes see Venus at dawn. It is the brightest planet, because it reflects the most light from the Sun.

A solar day on Venus is an amazing 5,832 hours long!

Sun

Mercury

Venus

Earth

Mars

Jupiter

Saturn

Uranus

Neptune

Earth

Earth is the only planet that contains liquid water. Because all living creatures need water to survive, it is believed to be the only planet supporting life.

Tons of **meteoroids** crash down into **Earth's atmosphere** each year. Scientists have even found rocks from Mars.

Earth has a **magnetic field**, which helps stop harmful **particles** from entering our atmosphere.

A day on Earth is 24 hours long. It may not be the fastest solar day, but it's definitely not the slowest!

Earth is sometimes called the *Blue Planet*, because nearly three-fourths of its surface is covered with water.

Sun

Mercury

Venus

Earth

Mars

Jupiter

Saturn

Uranus

Neptune

Mars

There is much less gravity on Mars than there is on Earth. If you were to jump on Mars, you would jump nearly three times higher!

Mars is known as the *Red Planet*. It appears red, because the dust and rocks on its surface contain a lot of iron.

A solar day on Mars is 25 hours long. That's just an hour longer than on Earth.

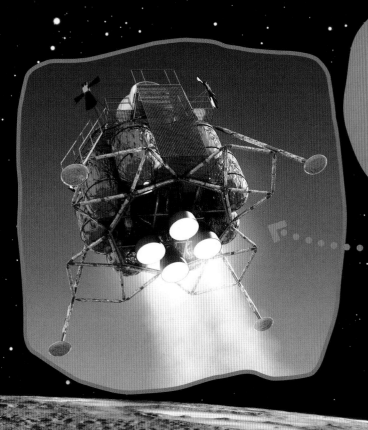

There have been many failed missions to Mars. It is a difficult place for a lander to touch down on with a heavy load!

No humans have visited Mars yet, but scientist have sent robotic machines to study it. These are called *Rovers*.

Sun

Mercury

Venus

Earth

Mars

Jupiter

Saturn

Uranus

Neptune

15

Jupiter

Jupiter is massive! It is twice as big as all of the other planets in the solar system put together.

More than 60 moons orbit Jupiter. It is also the fourth brightest natural object in the solar system.

The famous *Great Red Spot* is a giant storm, bigger than Earth, that has been raging for hundreds of years.

Jupiter is mostly made up of **gas**, which is swirled around by the great winds that circle the planet.

This giant planet has the shortest solar day, at just 10 hours long.

Sun

Mercury

Venus

Earth

Mars

Jupiter

Saturn

Uranus

Neptune

Saturn

Saturn is the fifth brightest object in our solar system. You will need a small telescope to see it from Earth.

Saturn is famous for its amazing rings, which are made of ice and dust that orbit the planet.

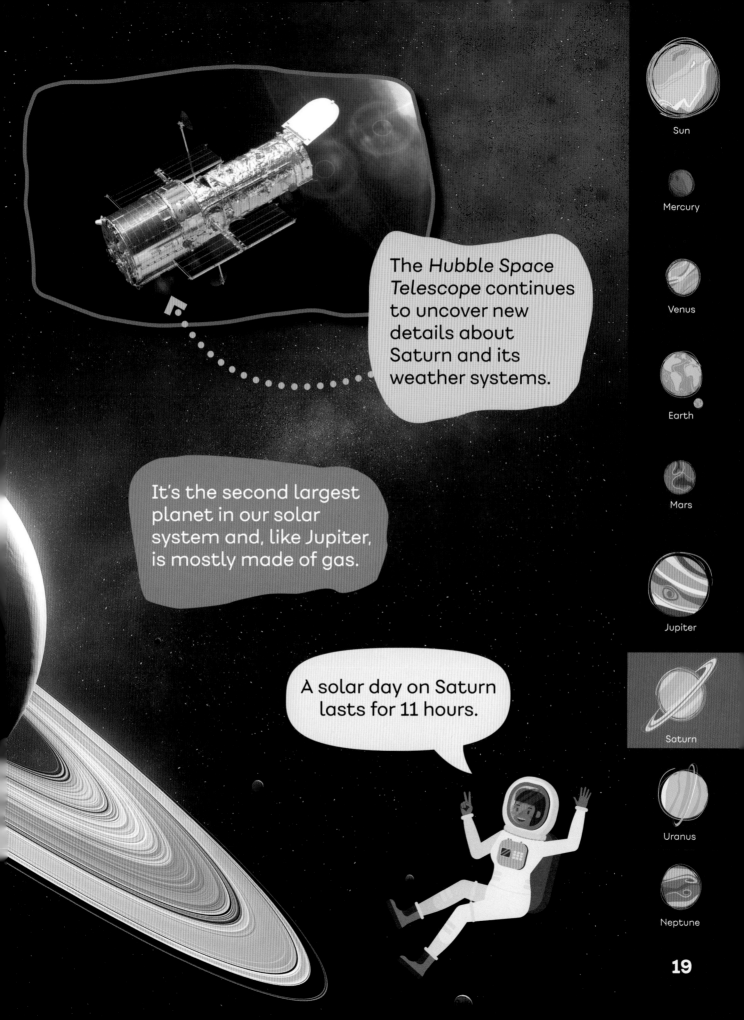

The *Hubble Space Telescope* continues to uncover new details about Saturn and its weather systems.

It's the second largest planet in our solar system and, like Jupiter, is mostly made of gas.

A solar day on Saturn lasts for 11 hours.

Sun

Mercury

Venus

Earth

Mars

Jupiter

Saturn

Uranus

Neptune

Uranus

Uranus is known as an *ice giant*. It was the first planet found with the help of a telescope, way back in 1781.

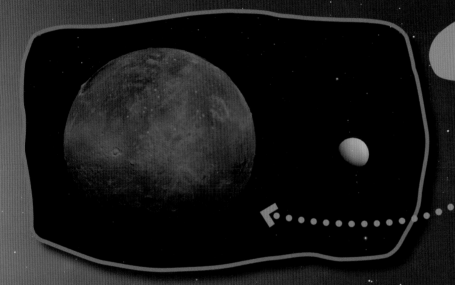

Uranus has 27 moons.

A solar day here is just 17 hours long.

This planet is a big ball of different gases. It probably would smell like rotten eggs there!

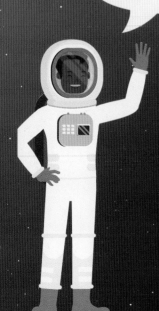

It is known as the
Sideways Planet,
because it rotates
on its side!

Sun

Mercury

Venus

Earth

Mars

Jupiter

Saturn

Uranus

Neptune

Neptune

Not only is Neptune the last planet in the solar system, it's also the windiest. It was first discovered in 1846.

Voyager 2 is the only spacecraft to have passed by this distant planet.

A solar day on this lonely planet is 16 hours long.

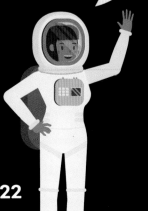

Neptune is 30 times farther away from the Sun than Earth. It is very dark and cold there!

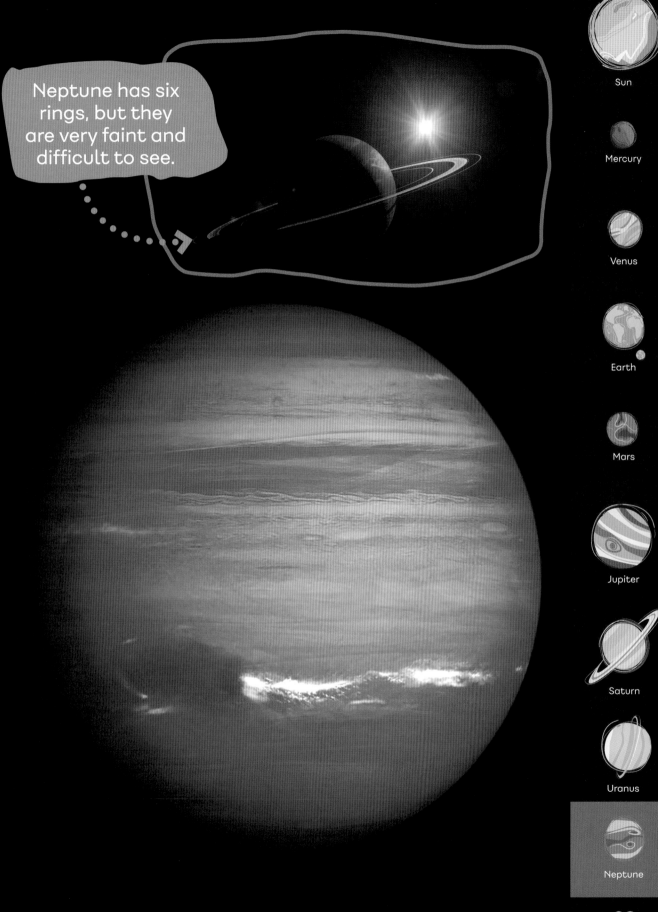

Neptune has six rings, but they are very faint and difficult to see.

Sun

Mercury

Venus

Earth

Mars

Jupiter

Saturn

Uranus

Neptune

Pluto and the Dwarf Planets

Pluto used to be known as the ninth and smallest planet in our solar system, but **astronomers** have now classed it as a *dwarf planet*.

Pluto lies in the Kuiper Belt, at the edge of our solar system, with a lot of icy rocky objects.

Pluto takes so long to orbit the Sun that you'd have to live there for 248 Earth years before going all the way around!

A solar day on Pluto is 153 hours long.

So far, four other dwarf planets have been discovered, but there could be many more.

In January 2006, NASA launched a robot spacecraft, *New Horizons*, to study the Kuiper Belt. It finally arrived at Pluto in July 2015. Now that is a very long journey!

The Sun and the Moon

The Sun provides light and heat to our whole solar system. Its light helps us see other moons and planets.

Our Moon is the brightest object in our night sky.

The Moon doesn't produce light. It looks bright, because it **reflects** light from the Sun.

Earth and our Moon are about 93 million miles (150 million km) from the Sun.

Scientists think the Moon was made when an object smashed into Earth. Pieces of our planet flew off into space, stuck together, and made the Moon!

27

The Sun

The Sun is very important to life on Earth. It provides energy to grow the plants that we need for food and **oxygen**. It also helps to keep us warm!

The Sun is so hot that there is nothing we can compare it to on Earth. Its middle can reach temperatures of 27 million °F (15 million °C).

The Sun is a star. Stars create heat and light. You can see a lot of stars in the sky, but they are all much farther away.

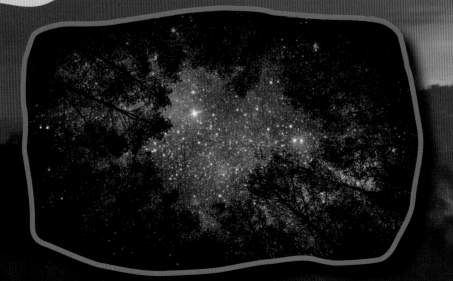

We use sunscreen to protect us from harmful rays from the Sun, which could damage our skin.

The Sun may look like fire, but it isn't. It's mostly made up of two kinds of gas: hydrogen and helium.

Earth's Orbit

It takes Earth 365 days to orbit the Sun, which is one whole year! You can't feel it, but Earth is zooming very quickly through space, even as you read this!

Earth is speeding around the Sun at about 18½ miles (30 km) per second. That's incredibly fast!

In one orbit, Earth will travel about 584 million miles (940 million km). Phew!

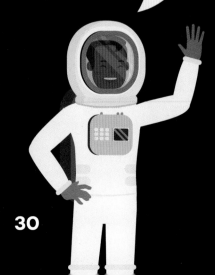

Earth orbits the Sun in an oval shape. This means that it is not always the same distance away from the Sun.

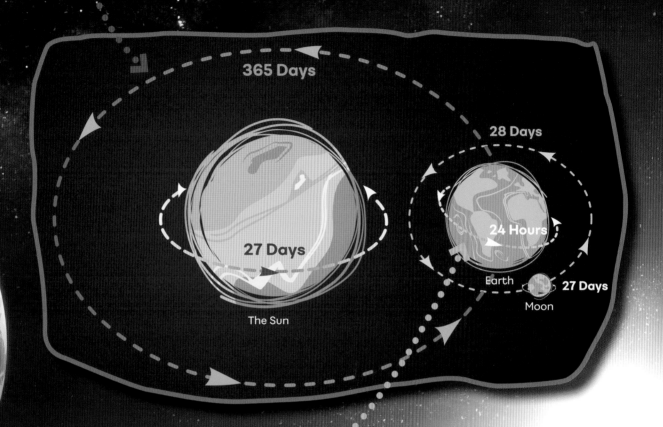

365 Days

28 Days

27 Days

24 Hours

The Sun

Earth

Moon

27 Days

While it orbits the Sun, Earth also spins around. It makes one full rotation every day.

The Moon

On July 20, 1969, *Neil Armstrong* and *Buzz Aldrin* became the first humans to set foot on the Moon, as part of the Apollo 11 mission.

Apollo 11 was launched by a Saturn V rocket from the Kennedy Space Center in Florida, USA, on July 16. It took 76 hours to enter orbit around the Moon.

We are still learning new things about the Moon. In 2020, NASA's mission SOFIA found proof that there is water on the Moon!

During their moon walk, Armstrong and Aldrin left a message that said, "We came in peace for all mankind."

The Moon's surface has mountains and a lot of **craters.** It is covered in powdery soil, pebbles and rocks.

The Moon's Orbit

As Earth orbits the Sun, the Moon travels around Earth. It takes 27 days for the Moon to complete its orbit.

As it orbits, the Moon appears to be different shapes when viewed from Earth. We call these shapes the *Phases of the Moon.*

The Moon has phases, because the Sun lights certain areas of the Moon at different stages of its orbit. From Earth, we see only the Sunlit parts.

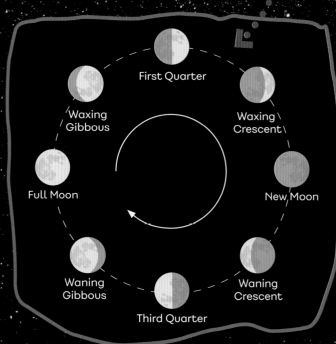

First Quarter

Waxing Gibbous

Waxing Crescent

Full Moon

New Moon

Waning Gibbous

Waning Crescent

Third Quarter

When Sunlight hits the Moon's surface, it can make it hot, with temperatures reaching 261°F (127°C).

The Moon's orbit affects the **tides** of our seas and oceans.

Day and Night

As Earth rotates, the Sun shines on the half of the planet that is facing it, providing it with daylight.

During the day, the Sun's energy keeps our planet warm and gives us **natural light**.

Because it is night in some parts of the world while it is day in others, different places have different **time zones**.

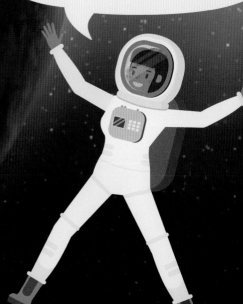

Sometimes you can see the Moon during daytime, too.

Seasons

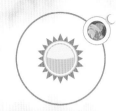

Most places on Earth have four seasons throughout the year. We experience changes to the light, weather and nature in each season, all because of the Sun!

EARTH'S TILTED AXIS

EQUATOR

Earth rotates at a tilted angle as it orbits the Sun. So, at different times of the year, some parts of Earth lean closer to the Sun and other parts will be farther away.

When part of Earth is leaning fully toward the Sun, it will be summer, and when it is leaning farthest away, it will be winter.

Some places don't have four seasons. Areas around the **equator** stay warm all year!

Eclipses

An eclipse occurs when an object in space, such as a moon or a planet, blocks another object from view. On Earth, we have *solar* and *lunar* eclipses.

A solar eclipse takes place when the Moon travels in front of the Sun, blocking some or all of it from view.

When the Sun is completely covered, we call it a *total eclipse*.

A lunar eclipse happens when the Sun, Moon and Earth are positioned in a straight line, with the Earth in the middle. Earth casts a shadow on the Moon, but it remains visible.

A lunar eclipse is sometimes called a *blood moon*, because it makes the Moon look red.

You should never look directly at a solar eclipse. It may look dark, but the Sun's rays can still damage your eyes!

Galaxies

A galaxy is a huge collection of dust, gas, stars and solar systems that are all held together by gravity. Our solar system is a small part of a galaxy known as the *Milky Way*.

There are about 30 other galaxies close to us. This is *Andromeda*, the closest major galaxy to the Milky Way.

In 1924, astronomer *Edwin Hubble* announced his discovery that the Milky Way was just one of many galaxies.

There could be as many as 100 billion galaxies, but we will need more powerful telescopes to see them.

The *James Webb Space Telescope* was launched into space in December 2021. It's the most powerful space telescope yet and will be able to take pictures of some of the first galaxies ever formed.

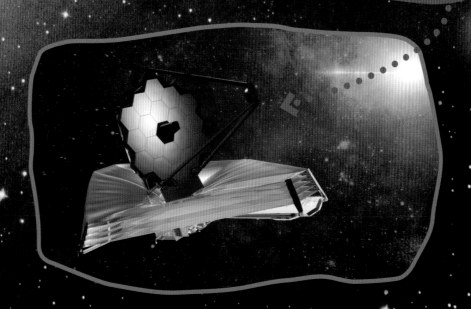

Stars

A star is a giant ball of hot gas called *plasma*, which is held together by its own gravity. There are hundreds of billions of stars in the Milky Way.

There are many different types of stars. *Red dwarfs* are the most common kind of star. They are smaller and cooler than our Sun.

The nearest star to Earth is the Sun, which is a *yellow dwarf*.

Shooting stars aren't stars at all! They are tiny pieces of dust and rock, called *meteoroids*, which burn up as they enter Earth's atmosphere.

VY Canis Majoris, the largest known star, is bigger than our Sun by at least 1,800 times!

How long a star lives depends on size. The larger the star, the shorter its life. A star like our Sun lives for about 10 billion years!

The Night Sky

There's a lot that can be discover about space without leaving Earth. For centuries, stargazers and astronomers have studied the stars that we can see in the night sky.

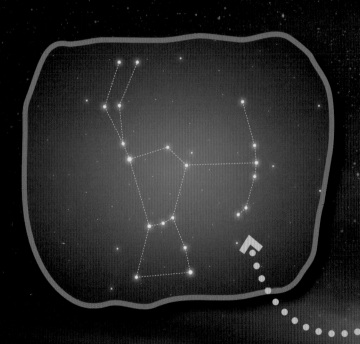

Constellations are groups of bright stars that stand out in the night sky. They form different shapes when you connect the dots.

This constellation is named *Orion*, after a great hunter from Greek myths. It looks like someone holding a bow and arrow.

Asteroids

Asteroids are rocky objects much smaller than planets, but they also orbit the Sun.

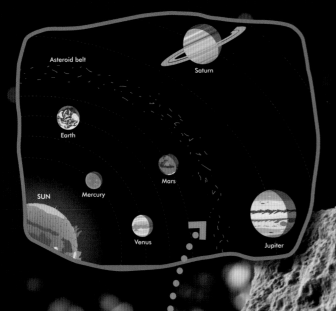

Asteroid belt

Saturn

Earth

Mars

Mercury

SUN

Venus

Jupiter

These rocks are leftover from the formation of our solar system.

Most asteroids are found in an area between the orbits of Mars and Jupiter, known as an *asteroid belt*.

Comets

Comets are space snowballs! They are made from ice, rock, dust and gases. Like asteroids, they also orbit the Sun.

Some comets are 15 times bigger than Earth!

Comets can sometimes be seen from Earth. When they get closer to the Sun, their ice and dust boils, which causes them to glow and makes them look like they have a tail.

The most famous comet is probably *Halley's Comet*, which can be seen from Earth every 74 to 76 years.

Get this in your calendar, Halley's Comet will return sometime in the year 2061.

Black Holes

Even without seeing one, astronomers know that black holes exist, because of the effect they have on objects that get close to them.

Most black holes are born when a giant star runs out of energy. The star collapses under its own weight, which causes an explosion called a *supernova*.

A black hole's gravity is so strong that it will pull in anything that gets too close, including light!

Nebulae

A nebula is a giant cloud of dust and gas in space! They are sometimes created from the dust thrown out by a supernova.

Our Sun was formed in a nebula.

Some **nebulae** are known as *star nurseries*, because they are where new stars are born!

One of the brightest is the *Orion Nebula*. It can sometimes be seen in the night sky.

Some nebulae, such as the *Eagle Nebula*, form strange, alien-like shapes.

Meteoroids

Small pieces of rock that travel through space are called *meteoroids*. If they enter a planet's atmosphere and burn up, they are then known as *meteors*.

When a lot of meteors fall at once, we call it a *meteor shower*. About 30 meteor showers can be seen from Earth each year.

Meteor showers happen when Earth travels through a stream of dust and rocks left by a passing comet.

Most meteors burn away before they can reach Earth's surface. Space rocks that make it to the ground are called *meteorites*.

Most meteorites are small rocks or pebbles. The largest meteorite found on Earth is the *Hoba* meteorite in Namibia.

Exploring Space

Space travel is a new science. It's been less than 100 years since the first spacecraft left Earth's atmosphere. There is still so much for us to explore and discover!

To see if it was safe to travel, animals were sent into space before humans.

A Russian dog named *Laika* was the first animal to completely orbit Earth in 1957. This statue in Moscow celebrates her important achievement.

The first human in space was Soviet **cosmonaut** *Yuri Gagarin*. On April 12, 1961, he completed one orbit of Earth in the spacecraft Vostok 1.

More than 5,000 spacecraft have been launched into space since 1957.

Spacecraft 🚀

A spacecraft is a vehicle or machine designed to travel into outer space. They are used for many different tasks, including collecting information, exploring planets, and transportation.

Building a spacecraft is very complicated. It can take up to 10 years to get one ready to launch.

A *lander* is a type of spacecraft that is designed to land on the surface of a planet or moon.

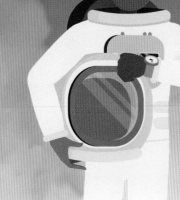

Space probes are robotic spacecraft that don't orbit Earth, but explore farther out into space instead.

Space *shuttles* were the first reusable spacecraft and were used to carry crew and **cargo** on 135 missions between 1981 and 2011.

Lift-Off!

During the countdown, scientists at mission control do final checks to make sure everything is working and that it's safe to launch.

Spacecraft and rockets are not the same thing. A rocket is used to carry a spacecraft outside of Earth's atmosphere.

Rockets carrying spacecraft usually take off from *launch-pads* at a *spaceport*.

After launching, parts of the rocket that are no longer needed for travel fall away in stages.

A rocket can reach a speed of 15,000 miles per hour (24,140 km/h) in as little as 8 minutes.

Race to the Moon

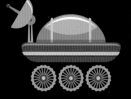

During the 1960s, the race was on between the USA and Soviet Union (USSR), as they competed to be the first country to send humans to the Moon.

In 1966, the Soviet spacecraft *Luna 9* was the first vehicle to land on the Moon. It took many photographs.

The USA won the race on July 20, 1969, when astronauts *Neil Armstrong* and *Buzz Aldrin* walked on the Moon for the first time. They stayed there for 21 hours 36 minutes.

The first footprints are probably still there, because there is no wind on the Moon to make them disappear.

Lunar Roving Vehicles (moon buggies) were taken to the Moon on later U.S. missions for astronauts to travel in. They are still on the Moon and belong to NASA.

Missions to Mars

Robotic spacecraft began observing Mars in the 1960s, looking for signs of life. No humans have visited Mars, yet!

Launches can be made only every two years, when Mars is closer to Earth (35 million miles/56 million km). It takes a lot of rocket fuel to reach Mars!

A number of martian rocks (meteorites from Mars) have fallen to Earth, so scientists have been able to study Mars without leaving our planet!

Mars Rovers are robotic vehicles that have been taken to Mars to send back information and images.

On July 30, 2020, Mars rover *Perseverance* was launched. Its mission is to seek signs of ancient life and collect rock samples. It can't return samples to Earth itself, so another spacecraft will have to be built to collect them.

Telescopes

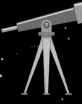

Telescopes are amazing inventions that let us see far out into space and discover new information about the stars, planets and other parts of our solar system.

Some telescopes have glass lenses that create magnified images. Very large telescopes are kept in buildings called *observatories*.

In 1609, the famous astronomer *Galileo* was the first person to see mountains and craters on the Moon through a telescope.

The James Webb Space Telescope can see a special type of light, called *infrared*, which is invisible to human eyes. It will let us see more of the universe than ever before.

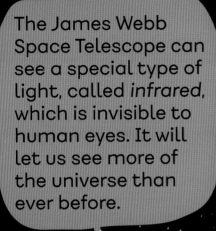

Radio telescopes are used to record the radio waves of space objects instead of images.

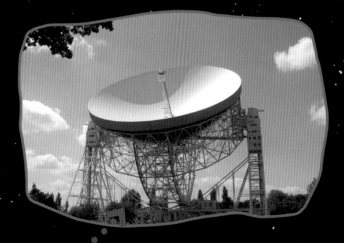

Is There Life Out There?

So far, no real evidence of life beyond our planet has been found, but many scientists believe we may not be alone in the universe.

To be able to support life, most scientists believe that a planet would need air, water, and the right amount of heat and light.

Scientists have sent radio messages into space, but so far there has been no response.

Mars used to be warmer and wetter than it is now, so it could have supported life. We continue to search for signs of tiny living things, such as **bacteria.**

There are thousands of other planets in our galaxy alone, so probably at least some of them could contain life. However, most of them are too far away for us to study properly.

International Space Station (ISS)

The ISS is a large spacecraft in orbit around Earth, It is home to crews of astronauts and cosmonauts.

Scientists are using the space station to learn more about living and working in space.

Spacecraft are used to take astronauts and cosmonauts to and from the ISS, and to deliver supplies.

There is zero gravity on board the ISS, which means that everything floats, unless it is secured, including the crew!

The ISS orbits Earth every 90 minutes and the people living there experience 16 sunrises a day!

Satellites

A satellite is something that orbits a planet or a star. The Moon is a satellite of Earth, and Earth is a satellite of the Sun.

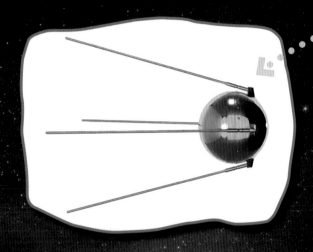

Sputnik 1 was the first **artificial satellite** to be launched into Earth's orbit in October 1957.

There are currently more than 2,000 active satellites orbiting Earth.

Artificial satellites are used for many purposes, including communications, **navigation** and predicting weather.

Many satellites are powered by solar panels, which collect energy from Sunlight.

What's Next?

There is so much of space left to be explored! Where will space travel take us next, and what will we discover along the way?

Space agencies are hoping to one day have a permanent base camp on the Moon.

Astronauts could be heading to Mars as soon as the 2030s!

New spacecraft, such as NASA's Space Launch System (SLS), will let astronauts travel deeper into space than ever before.

Space travel is very expensive, but scientists are working to create affordable and reusable spacecraft to let more people travel into space.

artificial satellite: A man-made satellite that is launched into space by humans.

astronomers: Scientists who study space.

bacteria: Tiny living things that can only be seen using a microscope.

cargo: Items or supplies carried by a vehicle.

cosmonaut: A Russian or Soviet astronaut.

craters: Large holes in the ground that have been caused by something hitting them or by explosions.

Earth's atmosphere: Layers of gases around Earth, which are held in place by gravity.

equator: An imaginary line around the middle of Earth's surface, at an equal distance between the North Pole and South Pole.

gas: A substance that is neither solid or liquid and has no fixed shape. Many gases are invisible.

gravity: A pulling force that works across space. It's the same force that causes an object to fall when you drop it.

magnetic field: An invisible space around a magnetic object.

meteoroids: Small natural objects, such as rocks or metals, that travel through outer space.

natural light: Light produced by the Sun.

navigation: To find your way from place to place.

nebulae: The plural name for nebula.

orbit: The path taken by one object circling around another object in space.

oxygen: A type of gas (see left) in the air that we need to breathe.

particles: Tiny pieces of something, such as specks of dust.

reflects: When light bounces off the surface of an object, it is reflected.

rotate (rotation): When something spins around its own central point. Earth makes one full rotation every day.

solar day: The time it takes for a planet to make one full rotation (see above), shifting from day to night as it moves in and out of the Sun's rays.

tides: The regular change in the level of the sea on the shore.

time zones: Areas of the world that are divided up according to what time they keep. Some time zones are behind or ahead of others by multiple hours.

Index

Picture Credits
(abbreviations: t = top; b = bottom; m = middle; l = left; r = right; bg = background)

Shutterstock: Dima Zel 2bg; Vadim Sadovski 4bg; Love the Wind 4bl; Vadim Sadovski 6bg; Vadim Sadovski 8bg; Blue Crayola 10bg; Astrostar 11tr; Vibrant image studio 12bg; Mopic 12b; Triff 13t; Jurik Peter 14bg; 3D Sculptor 15tl; Triff 15ml; Vadim Sadovski 16bg; Dotted Yeti 16bl; Johan Swanepoel 18bg; Dotted Yeti 19tl; Vadim Sadovski 20bg; Aleksandr Morrisovich 20ml; Tristan 3D 22bg; Dotted Yeti 22ml; Dotted Yeti 23tr; Vadim Sadovski 24bg; NASA Images 24m; Edobric 25br; Aphelleon 26bg; Sahara Prince 26br; Gilda Villarreal 28bg; Triff 28b; Vadim Sadovski 30bg; Grayjay 31m; Dima Zel 32bg; Everett Collection 32bl; Baranov 34bg; Flash Movie 36bg; Siberia art 36bl; Lijphoto 37br; Elena Zajchikova 38bg; Yaska 38ml; Designua 39tr; Romolo Tavani 40bg; Azstarman 41ml; Fred Mantel 41tr; Mohamed Eikhamisy 42bg; Dotted Yeti 43bm; Jurik Peter 44bg; BJ Nartker 45tr; Paklista 46bg; Ad_Hominem 46ml; Dabarti CGI 48bg; Blue Bee 48ml; Paul Fleet 50bg; Brian Donovan 51mr; Vahal 52bg; NASA Images 52ml; Maximillion Laschon 53tr; Pike-28 54bg; Antares-starexplorer 55tl; Mohamed Eikhamisy 55br; Vadim Sadovski 56bg; Sky2020 56mr; Rostasedlacek 57br; Rangizzz 58bg; Asetta 58bl; Arkady Mazor 59mr; Dima Zel 60bg; Castleski 60ml; Solarseven 61tr; Kent Weakley 62bg; Crystal eye Studio 63tm; Sirko-Herr 64bg; Aleks49 64ml; Digital Images Studio 65tl; Castleski 65bl; Paopano 66bg; Vadim Sadovski 66mr; Olivier LAURENT Photos 68bg; Bill Anastasiou 68mr; Andrew Barker 69br; Kerem Gogus 70bg; Merlin74 71ml; Vadim Sadovski 72bg; Tatiana Shepeleva 74bg; Woverwolf 74ml; Johan Swanepoel 74br; 3000ad 76bg; 3D Sculptor 77tl; Sefart 78bg; Vadim Sadovski 80bg.

Every effort has been made to trace the copyright holders and we apologize in advance for any unintentional omissions. We would be pleased to insert the appropriate credit in any subsequent edition of this publication.